Vegan Salads

Delicious and Nutritious, Super Easy & Fast, Fruit, Veggie and Superfood Salad Recipes for a Healthy Plant-Based Lifestyle

By Karen Greenvang

Copyright ©Karen Greenvang 2019

All rights reserved. No part of this publication may be reproduced, stored in a retrieval system, or transmitted, in any form or by any means, electronic, mechanical, photocopying, recording or otherwise, without the prior written permission of the author and the publishers.

Sign Up for Karen's Free Vegan Newsletter Today:

Karen's Best Vegan Tips, Inspiration, Awesome Recipes Resources and New Releases to Help You Live a Balanced Vegan Lifestyle:

www.YourWellnessBooks.com/karen

The scanning, uploading, and distribution of this book via the Internet, or via any other means, without the permission of the author is illegal and punishable by law. Please purchase only authorized electronic editions, and do not participate in or encourage electronic piracy of copyrighted materials.

Copyright @ 2019 Karen Greenvang, All Rights Reserved

All information in this book has been carefully researched and checked for factual accuracy. However, the author and publishers make no warranty, expressed or implied, that the information contained herein is appropriate for every individual, situation or purpose, and assume no responsibility for errors or omission. The reader assumes the risk and full responsibility for all actions, and the author will not be held liable for any loss or damage, whether consequential, incidental, and special or otherwise, that may result from the information presented in this publication.

All cooking is an experiment in a sense, and many people come to the same or similar recipe over time. All recipes in this book have been derived from author's personal experience. Should any bear a close resemblance to those used elsewhere, that is purely coincidental.

The book is not intended to provide medical advice or to take the place of medical advice and treatment from your personal physician. Readers are advised to consult their own doctors or other qualified health professionals regarding the treatment of medical conditions. If you suffer from any health issues, are pregnant or on medication, we recommend you consult with your physician.

The author shall not be held liable or responsible for any misunderstanding or misuse of the information contained in this book. The information is not intended to diagnose, treat or cure any disease.

It is important to remember that the author of this book is not a doctor/ medical professional. Only opinions based upon her own personal experiences or research are cited. THE AUTHOR

DOES NOT OFFER MEDICAL ADVICE or prescribe any treatments. For any health or medical issues – you should be talking to your doctor first.

This recipe book is designed as an inspirational guide to motivate you to live a healthy lifestyle but should not be interpreted as a resource to treat serious health conditions.

Contents

Introduction 11

About the Recipes & the Measurements 17

Recipe # 1 Papaya Pineapple Protein Morning Energizer 18

Recipe #2 Very Berry-licious Breakfast or Snack 19

Recipe #3 Banana Romance Superfood Sweet Salad 20

Recipe #4 Vitamin C Iron Energy Salad 21

Recipe #5 Apple and Apple Cider Nutritional Mix 22

Recipe #6 Banana Grape Green Dream 23

Recipe #7 Apple Carrot Dream 24

Recipe #8 Date Nut Date 25

Recipe #9 Brazil Nuts Quick Detox Salad 26

Recipe #10 Warm-Up Salad Recipe 27

Recipe #11 Fresh Cilantro Delight 29

Recipe #12 Easy Mediterranean Salad 30

Recipe #13 Herbal Green Dream Salad 31

Recipe #14 Orange Dream Summer Salad 33

Recipe #15 Hydrating Green Detox Salad 34

Recipe #16 Mediterranean Baby Spinach Salad 35

Recipe #17 Delicious Pumpkin Surprise 37

Recipe #18 Raw Almost Green Energy Boost Salad 38

Recipe #19 Nourishing Herbal Avocado Salad 39

Recipe #20 Chili Papaya Salad 40

Recipe #21 Pineapple Crunchy Protein Salad 41

Recipe #22 Arugula Pears Seduction Salad .. 42

Recipe #23 Iceberg Hydration Salad 43

Recipe #24 Oriental Creamy Iceberg Dream 44

Recipe #25 Green Protein Salad 45

Recipe #26 Sweet Pepper Dream 46

Recipe #27 Creamy Spinach Strawberry Salad 47

Recipe #28 Easy Red Cabbage Grape Salad .. 48

Recipe #29 Tasty Dinner Vegan Ratatouille . 49

Recipe #30 Quinoa Curry Salad 51

Recipe #31 Comfort Sweet Potato Salad 52

Recipe #32 Easy Tomato Salad 53

Recipe #33 Avocado's Walnut Mix 54

Recipe #34 Avocado Strawberries Salad 55

Recipe #35 Aromatic Soy Sprouts Salads 56

Recipe #36 Stuffed Zucchini Salad 57

Recipe #37 Natural Detox Recipe 58

Recipe #38 Spicy Exotic Salad 59

Recipe #39 Spicy Raw Veggie Noodles 60

Recipe #40 Summer Salsa Salad 61

Recipe #41 Spice It Up Papaya Salad 63

Recipe #42 Easy Chia Snack Salad 64

Recipe #43 Tantalizing Thai Salad 65

Recipe #44 Carrot & Cucumber in Spicy Green Salsa 66

Recipe #45 Easy Ginger Almond Salad 67

Recipe #46 Beautiful Skin Salad with a Coconut Dressing 68

Recipe #47 Spicy Pepper Salad 69

Recipe #48 Recycle Salad with Vegan Coco Yoghurt Dip 71

Recipe #49 Fresh Basil Potato Salad 72

Recipe #50 Detox Pomegranate 3 Ingredient Salad 73

Recipe #51 Quick Quinoa Salad 74
Recipe #52 Arugula Lentil Salad with Lemon Parsley Dressing 75
Recipe #53 Black Beans & Olive Salad 76
Recipe #54 Roasted Broccoli Salad................ 77
Recipe #55 Smoked Tofu and Sweet Potato Green Salad.. 78
Recipe #56 Easy Artichoke Detox Salad 79
Recipe #57 No More Sugar Cravings Salad 80
Recipe #58 Easy Quinoa Salad........................... 81
Recipe #1 Comfort Wellness Smoothie........ 83
Recipe #2 Digestive Smoothie.......................... 84
Recipe #3 Beauty Balance Smoothie 85
Recipe #4 Protein Smoothie............................. 86
Recipe #5 Flaxseed Protein Smoothie 87
Recipe #6 Homemade Trail Mix....................... 88
Recipe #7 Green Nutrition Smoothie 89
Recipe #8 Soothing Lavender Pegan Smoothie 90
Recipe #9 Nutritious Vanilla Smoothie.......... 91
Recipe #10 Herbal Coconut Smoothie 92
In Conclusion... 94

Special Offer from Karen- VIP Reader Newsletter.. 95

More Books Written by Karen Greenvang..... 96

Vegan Salads - Introduction

Introduction

Thank you so much for taking an interest in this book.

It really means a lot to me!

My name is Karen. A few years ago, I decided to transition to a vegan plant-based lifestyle and it really transformed my health and all areas of my life.

After going through my own radical transformation, I have made it my passion and purpose to help others enrich their lives with healing, vegan, plant-based foods. The book you're holding in your hands is one of the fruits of my mission to help you on your health and wellness journey by giving you simple to follow recipes and inspiration.

Why I wrote this book?

After surveying my readers, I have quickly identified that most of them were looking for quick and easy recipes. Something "simple to follow". It made so much sense to me.

Vegan salads are the best solution, because they can be created quickly and easily, even if a person is not an experienced chef.

The best part? You can conjure up all kinds of salads.

We are talking tasty, delicious and nutritious plant-based salads you will never get bored with. Salads that are healing and rich in natural protein while offering a variety of taste,

Vegan Salads - Introduction

from spicy to sweet. Some salads can also be served as a quick snack.

Whether you are just starting out, or are a vegan veteran looking for new recipes, or perhaps you want to start eating less of processed foods while adding an abundance of healing, nutrient rich recipes- you have come to the right place.

Some recipes are fully raw, some are slightly cooked. They are designed for you to pick and choose. With 58 salad recipes, as well as 10 bonus recipes, you will surely find at least a few recipes to add to your healthy collection.

My mistakes with a vegan diet

I'll be honest with you because I am not ashamed of admitting my mistakes. We are in this together and it is my hope that by admitting what I did wrong with my diet you can avoid my early mistakes.

When I first got started on a vegan diet, I ate way too many processed foods. I was happy I stopped eating animal products, however I did not make any effort to learn about balanced vegan nutrition. And I still hated eating veggies.

So I was living on a vegan junk food, sugar, processed carbs, coffee and soda.

Because of that, I was feeling tired all the time. It was only when I started transitioning to a fresh, plant-based, unprocessed diet, that I was able to create unstoppable energy through a balanced, whole food vegan diet.

Vegan Salads - Introduction

And it's thanks to that "unstoppable energy" I can use my free time to create vegan plant-based recipe guides like this one.

Every now and then, I still treat myself to vegan junk food. It's absolutely fine as a treat.

But, it feels good to know I have my balanced, vegan, plant-based plan to follow and a foundation that is fresh, clean, vegan diet that helps me revitalize my mind and body. I no longer need to drink coffee to keep me going. I drink it every now and then because I enjoy it. However, I no longer need it to function as a normal human being.

The good news? You can get hooked on healthy eating, fruits, veggies and superfoods. When you start adding vegan salads to your diet, your mindset and habits will start shifting. Your body will feel happy because you will be feeding it vital nutrients it needs to stimulate the healing process and give you the nutrition you deserve to create the new, healthier and more empowered you.

Even some of the meat eaters in my family decided to give a vegan plant-based diet a try because of the easy to follow and delicious recipes I share in this guide.

This book is an excellent choice for:

-vegans and vegetarians
-healthy eating lovers
-anyone interested in a plant-based lifestyle
-anyone wishing to add more fresh fruits and vegetables into their diets
-gluten-free diet followers

Vegan Salads - Introduction

-anyone wishing to eat more alkaline foods to restore natural energy

The beauty of these recipes is that they create meals that are very easy to have on the go since they consist of such simple and basic ingredients.

If you feel sick and tired of feeling sick and tired and wish to restore energy and zest for life, try to add more vegan salads to your diet.

At the same time, remember to drink plenty of water and eliminate, or reduce, caffeine and sugar drinks.

Even if you eat this way 80% of the time, you will still be able to energize yourself.

The role of alkaline foods

By eating more fresh vegetables and fruits you help your body work at its optimal level.

You see, our blood's optimal pH should be 7.365- which is slightly alkaline. By adding more alkaline foods (such as fresh fruits and veggies that are naturally rich in vitamins and minerals) we help our body regulate its optimal blood pH.

Alkaline foods are plant-based, unprocessed, low in sugar, and high in mineral and vitamin content. All veggies are highly alkalizing, and so are the leafy greens, herbs, and low sugar fruits.

Vegan Salads - Introduction

Acid forming foods are foods that are processed, contain sugar and gluten, as well as nasty chemicals. Animal products are acid-forming too.

If we fail to nourish ourselves with a diet that is rich in alkaline foods, and we eat processed foods that are acid-forming, we torture our body with incredible stress. If we constantly eat foods that are acid-forming, we eventually get sick as our body can no longer regulate its pH for us. The diet rich in vegan salads is naturally alkaline-forming and helps us restore energy.

It is my hope that you will find at least a few recipes you will love and add to your favorite, vegan on-the go recipes to enjoy on a busy day.

To your health and wellbeing,

Enjoy!

For more inspiration & empowerment join my VIP email newsletter and start receiving my best vegan tips & recipes to help you transition to a healthy, vegan lifestyle.

Visit the link below to sign up, it's free:

www.YourWellnessBooks.com/karen

I hope to "see you" inside ☺

Vegan Salads - Introduction

Delicious Vegan Salad Recipes Including Fruit, Veggie, Herb and Superfood Salads

Vegan Salads - Introduction

About the Recipes & the Measurements

The cup measurement I use is the American Cup measurement.

I also use it for dry ingredients. If you are new to it, let me help you:

If you don't have American Cup measures, just use a metric or imperial liquid measuring jug and fill your jug with your ingredient to the corresponding level. Here's how to go about it:

1 American Cup= 250ml= 8 fl.oz.

For example:

If a recipe calls for 1 cup of almonds, simply place your almonds into your measuring jug until it reaches the 250 ml/8oz mark.

I hope you found it helpful. I know that different countries use different measurements and I wanted to make things simple for you. I have also noticed that very often those who are used to American Cup measurements complain about metric measurements and vice versa. However, if you apply what I have just explained, you will find it easy to use both.

Now, let's dive into the recipes!

Delicious Vegan Salad Recipes

Recipe # 1 Papaya Pineapple Protein Morning Energizer

Pineapples are well known for their anti-inflammatory benefits and high vitamin C content. Papaya adds even more natural Vitamin C content as well as antioxidants and the essential minerals: potassium, copper and magnesium. We are taking this recipe to the next level by adding some natural protein and good fats from brazil nuts and chia seeds. Coconut milk and cinnamon powder make this recipe truly irresistible while quinoa will help you stay full and focused till lunch. This recipe is also great as a mid-afternoon snack.

Serves: 2
Ingredients:
- Half cup of fresh papaya, diced
- Half cup of fresh pineapple, diced
- Handful of raw brazil nuts, roughly chopped
- 2 tablespoons of chia seed powder
- 6 tablespoons of cooked quinoa
- 1 teaspoon of cinnamon powder
- 1/4 cup of thick coconut milk (you can replace it with any other vegan friendly milk of your choice)

Instructions:
1. In a salad bowl mix the diced papaya and pineapple together.
2. Sprinkle the brazil nuts and quinoa over the top.
3. Sprinkle the chia seeds and cinnamon powder.
4. Toss all the ingredients.
5. Pour over the coconut milk and mix well. Enjoy!

Delicious Vegan Salad Recipes

Recipe #2 Very Berry-licious Breakfast or Snack

This recipe is a great way to sneak in some leafy greens.

Berries are very high in antioxidants and essential minerals. The cashews add the protein, essential fats, as well as creamy, delicious taste you will get hooked on.

Serves: 2
Ingredients:
- ¼ cup of fresh strawberries, chopped
- ¼ cup of fresh raspberries
- ¼ cup of fresh blueberries
- 1 handful of baby spinach leaves, chopped
- a few fresh mint leaves
- ¼ cup of raw unsalted cashews roughly chopped
- 4 tablespoons of thick coconut milk
- Optional: stevia, maple syrup, or a few banana slices to sweeten

Instructions:
1. Mix all the berries together in a small salad bowl or dessert bowl.
2. Add in the baby spinach leaves and toss well.
3. Sprinkle the roughly chopped cashews over the berries.
4. Pour over coconut milk and mix well.
5. If needed, sweeten with stevia, maple syrup or a few banana slices.
6. Serve with fresh mint leaves. Enjoy!

Delicious Vegan Salad Recipes

Recipe #3 Banana Romance Superfood Sweet Salad

Who said that all salads must be green vegetable salads? Fruit salads are also delicious and nutritious. Bananas are high in potassium and energy. They are a very good breakfast choice as they provide a healthy dose of nutrient rich carbohydrate. Maca powder and chia seeds will help you stay focused and feel energized for hours. Blueberries add to anti-inflammatory properties and coconut oil makes this creative salad taste delicious. Pecan nuts are known for their protein content as well as their ability to lower bad cholesterol.

Serves: 1-2
Ingredients:
- 1 large banana, sliced
- 1 tablespoon of raw pecan nuts, roughly chopped
- Half cup of fresh blueberries
- ¼ teaspoon maca powder
- Half teaspoon cinnamon
- 2 tablespoons melted coconut oil
- 1 tablespoon cocoa powder

Instructions:
1. Place the sliced banana and blueberries in a serving bowl. Sprinkle the chopped pecan nuts
2. Sprinkle the maca powder and cinnamon.
3. In a separate bowl, combine melted coconut oil with cocoa powder. Mix well.
4. Pour the coconut oil cocoa mixture over your fruit salad.
5. Place in a fridge for 15- 30 minutes. Serve and enjoy!

Delicious Vegan Salad Recipes

Recipe #4 Vitamin C Iron Energy Salad

Citrus fruits are known for their high vitamin C and antioxidant properties, and spinach is a natural source of iron. This recipe is just perfect for boosting your immune system. The seeds used in this recipe are high in healthy omega 3 fats and provide a good source of energy.

Serves: 1-2
Ingredients:
- 2 medium sized oranges, peeled and divided into smaller pieces
- 1 medium sized grapefruit, peeled and divided into smaller pieces
- 1 tablespoon of raw seed mix of your choice
- 1 tablespoon of raisins
- Half cup of fresh baby spinach
- Half cup of fresh arugula leaves
- 1 teaspoon of cinnamon
- Half lime
- 2 tablespoons of maple syrup

Instructions:
1. Place the greens in a salad bowl and pour over 2 tablespoons of maple syrup. Mix well so that all the leaves absorb the maple syrup.
2. Add the oranges and grapefruit.
3. Sprinkle the raw seeds over the grapefruit and orange.
4. Sprinkle the cinnamon.
5. Toss together and serve with fresh lime juice. Enjoy!

Delicious Vegan Salad Recipes

Recipe #5 Apple and Apple Cider Nutritional Mix

Apples are very rich in essential anti-oxidants and blend very well with pears. Cashew nuts provide protein, essential minerals and healthy fats. Apple cider vinegar helps stimulate natural weight loss and it's also believed to kill harmful bacteria. Nutritional yeast adds in more nutrients that are essential if you want to create a healthy and sustainable vegan lifestyle.

Serves: 2-3
Ingredients:
- 1 big red apple, cored and sliced
- 1 big green apple, cored and sliced
- 2 pears, sliced
- 1 handful of raw cashew nuts, roughly chopped
- 1 tablespoon of apple cider vinegar
- 1 teaspoon of cinnamon powder
- 1 tablespoon nutritional yeast
- 2 tablespoons raw cashew milk
- Half teaspoon brown sugar or cane sugar

Instructions:
1. Place the apples and pears in a serving bowl.
2. Sprinkle the chopped cashew nuts.
3. In a separate bowl, combine the apple cider vinegar, raw cashew milk, cinnamon powder, nutritional yeast and sugar. Mix well.
4. Now spread the mixture over the apple pear mix.

Delicious Vegan Salad Recipes

Recipe #6 Banana Grape Green Dream

Grapes are high in essential minerals and vitamin C, and make this salad incredibly sweet. Pistachios are high in protein, essential fats and fiber.

Avocado is a highly alkalizing fruit and is an amazing source of Magnesium and good fats.

Serves: 2-3
Ingredients:
- 1 big banana, peeled and sliced
- 4 tablespoons thick coconut milk
- Half cup green grapes, halved
- Half cup red grapes, halved
- Handful of raw pistachio nuts, roughly chopped
- 1 big avocado, peeled, pitted and sliced
- A handful of fresh cilantro
- Pinch of cinnamon powder

Instructions;
1. Place all the dry ingredients in a salad bowl and toss well.
2. Sprinkle over some coconut milk and cinnamon powder.
3. Mix well, serve and enjoy!

Delicious Vegan Salad Recipes

Recipe #7 Apple Carrot Dream

This recipe creates a unique taste by combining apples, carrots and red bell peppers which are very high in anti-oxidants and help alkalize the body.

It's a great beginner recipe and it's just perfect for people looking for tasty ways of adding more veggies to their diets.

Serves: 1-2
Ingredients:
- 1 big green apple, peeled, and sliced
- 4 carrots, peeled and sliced
- 1 big red bell pepper, sliced
- Handful of raw almonds, soaked in water for a few hours
- 1 tablespoon avocado oil
- Juice of half a lemon

Instructions:
1. Combine all the ingredients in a salad bowl.
2. Mix well.
3. Sprinkle over some avocado oil and fresh lemon juice.
4. Toss and serve!
5. Enjoy!

Delicious Vegan Salad Recipes

Recipe #8 Date Nut Date

Thanks to the low glycemic and high fiber properties of apples, along with the natural, plant-based protein provided by the hazel nuts, this is a great salad recipe for breakfast.

It's also great as a quick snack or a post workout salad.

Serves: 1-2
Ingredients:
- 2 small apples (of your choice) cored and sliced
- 10 dates, pitted
- 20 raw hazel nuts
- Juice of half a lemon
- 2 tablespoons of coconut shavings

Instructions:
1. Place all the ingredients in a salad bowl.
2. Mix well and sprinkle over some lemon juice.
3. Enjoy!

Delicious Vegan Salad Recipes

Recipe #9 Brazil Nuts Quick Detox Salad

This recipe is a fantastic detox recipe as it's full of fresh, alkalizing ingredients and full of healing vitamins and minerals. Treat yourself to this salad whenever you need to balance your energy levels and give your body what it needs to stimulate massive healing.

Serves: 2
Ingredients:
- 2 big cucumbers, peeled and sliced
- A handful or radish, halved
- A small garlic clove, minced
- A handful of raw Brazil nuts, roughly chopped
- 2 big tomatoes, sliced and peeled
- Juice of half lime
- 1 teaspoon of olive or avocado oil
- Himalaya salt to taste
- Pinch of black pepper to taste

Instructions:
1. Place the cucumbers, radish and tomatoes in a salad bowl.
2. Add the Brazil nuts and garlic.
3. Sprinkle over some olive oil, lime juice, Himalaya salt and black pepper to taste.
4. Toss well and enjoy!

Delicious Vegan Salad Recipes

Recipe #10 Warm-Up Salad Recipe

Tomatoes are high in vitamin C, beta-carotene, anti-oxidants and essential minerals such as potassium. Mushrooms offer a fantastic source of selenium and vitamin D. Avocados are highly alkalizing and they contain potassium and essential fats.

Serves: 2-4
Ingredients:
- Half cup of cherry tomatoes, halved
- Half cup of white button mushrooms
- Half cup of black mushrooms
- 1 teaspoon of fresh garlic, finely chopped
- 1 teaspoon of fresh rosemary
- 1 ripe avocado, halved and pitted
- 1 tablespoon extra-virgin olive oil
- 1 tablespoon raw pistachio nuts, roughly chopped

Instructions:
1. Heat the olive oil in a saucepan.
2. Add the garlic and rosemary, fry until the garlic has softened.
3. Add the mushrooms and turn the heat down to a medium one, cover the saucepan with its lid and allow the mushrooms to reduce.
4. Once the mushrooms have started boiling in their own water, remove the lid from the saucepan and allow all the liquid to cook off the mushrooms.
5. Once the mushrooms begin to brown, add the tomatoes and cook at a medium/high heat until both the

Delicious Vegan Salad Recipes

mushrooms and tomatoes have browned and cooked through.
6. Place the avocado halves on a plate and fill each half with the mushroom and tomato mixture.
7. Sprinkle the chopped pistachios over the stuffed avocado halves and serve.
8. Enjoy!

Delicious Vegan Salad Recipes

Recipe #11 Fresh Cilantro Delight

This vegetable salad provides a healthy dose of vitamins, minerals and fiber. Cilantro – coconut milk salsa makes this salad super creamy and tasty. The seeds added offer a healthy dose of fats. The cashew nuts provide the natural vegan protein.

Serves: 2-4
Ingredients:
- Half cup of fresh cilantro, washed
- Half cup of cherry tomatoes, halved
- 2 fresh cucumbers, peeled and sliced
- 2 carrots, peeled and sliced
- Half cup of raw green beans, julienned
- Half cup of mung bean sprouts
- 1 tablespoon of raw seed mix
- 1 tablespoon of raw cashew nuts, whole
- Himalaya salt to taste
- A few lemon slices to serve

Instructions:
1. On a serving plate, place the fresh cilantro.
2. Top with the mung bean sprouts, cherry tomatoes, cucumbers, carrots and green beans.
3. Sprinkle over the raw seeds and cashew nuts.
4. Season with Himalaya salt if needed.
5. Serve with a few lemon slices to garnish.
6. Enjoy!

Delicious Vegan Salad Recipes

Recipe #12 Easy Mediterranean Salad

This salad is more than just a "green salad". It's a simple yet sophisticated blend of healing Mediterranean spices, and unique taste you will surely get hooked on. The best part? It's very easy to make.

Serves: 2-3
Ingredients:
- Half cup of fresh basil leaves
- 1 cup of fresh cherry tomatoes, halved
- 1 cup of arugula leaves
- A handful of baby spinach leaves
- Half cup of black olives, pitted
- Half cup of green olives, pitted
- ¼ cup of raw pine nuts
- 1 tablespoon of olive oil
- Himalaya salt to taste.
- Optional: vegan feta cheese

Instructions:
1. In a salad bowl combine the fresh basil leaves, cherry tomatoes, arugula leaves, handful of spinach leaves, olives and pine nuts.
2. Toss well. Add some vegan feta cheese if needed.
3. Now, sprinkle over some olive oil and Himalaya salt to taste if needed.
4. Toss again, serve and enjoy!

Delicious Vegan Salad Recipes

Recipe #13 Herbal Green Dream Salad

Arugula is high in essential minerals and dietary fiber; it also has a unique mustardy flavor that makes it a great base for any salad. It tastes much nicer than spinach or kale (in my opinion).

Eggplant is a great source of vitamin B1 and manganese. In this case the eggplant must be cooked prior to preparing this salad, as it is not a vegetable that is particularly palatable when raw.

Personally, I am a big fan of balance and combing raw foods with cooked foods and this recipe reflects just that.

Serves: 2-4
Ingredients:
- 1 cup arugula leaves
- 1 small eggplant, sliced
- 1 tablespoon Mediterranean herb mix (for example rosemary and thyme)
- 1 cup cherry tomatoes, halved
- 2 fresh cucumbers, peeled and sliced
- Half cup raw green beans, julienned
- Handful of raw brazil nuts, roughly chopped
- Half of ripe avocado, pitted and sliced

Instructions to cook the eggplant:
1. Preheat the oven to 350 degrees Fahrenheit (=200 degrees Celsius).
2. Lay the eggplant slices on a non-stick baking sheet.
3. Sprinkle with the mixed dried herbs.

Delicious Vegan Salad Recipes

4. Cook for approximately 20 minutes, or until the egg plant slices begin to brown.
5. Once cooked, transfer to a cooling rack to cool while you begin preparing the rest of the salad

Instructions to make the salad:
1. In a salad bowl, combine arugula with the cherry tomatoes, cucumber, green beans and cooled eggplant slices.
2. Place the sliced avocado over the top.
3. Now, sprinkle the chopped Brazil nuts over the top of the salad and serve.
4. Enjoy!

Delicious Vegan Salad Recipes

Recipe #14 Orange Dream Summer Salad

The unique combination of carrot and orange in this salad provides an abundance of vitamin C, fiber, beta-carotene, antioxidants as well as a unique flavor.

Dates add to the natural sweetness of this salad and hazelnuts and chia seeds enrich it with natural protein and good fats. It's one of my favorite take-away salads to enjoy on the beach. This recipe is called the Orange Dream Summer Salad for a reason.

Serves: 2
Ingredients:
- 5 raw carrots, peeled and grated
- 3 oranges, peeled and segmented
- Handful of dates, pitted
- Handful of hazelnuts
- 2 tablespoons chia seeds
- Pinch of cinnamon powder
- 2 tablespoons thick coconut milk

Instructions:
1. Place the grated carrot and oranges in a salad bowl.
2. Add the dates and sprinkle over the hazelnuts and chia seeds.
3. Pour over 2 tablespoons of thick coconut milk.
4. Mix well, season with cinnamon powder and enjoy!

Recipe #15 Hydrating Green Detox Salad

Cucumber and apple are a wonderful and amazingly hydrating combination. The low glycemic index of the apples will help you sustain your energy and stave off hunger until dinner time.

Serves: 1-2
Ingredients
- 2 small green apples, cored and sliced
- ¼ cup raw pecan nuts, roughly chopped
- 2 cucumbers, peeled and sliced
- 1 tablespoon of fresh lime juice
- A handful of raisins
- Optional: thick coconut milk (about 4 tablespoons)

Instructions:
1. Place the apple slices on a serving plate.
2. Drizzle over the lime juice in order to stop the apple from browning.
3. Add the chopped pecan nuts, raisins and cucumbers.
4. Sprinkle over some coconut milk if needed.

Delicious Vegan Salad Recipes

Recipe #16 Mediterranean Baby Spinach Salad

You already know that leafy greens are good for you. The question is how to actually add more leafy greens to your diet and make it a fun habit? This recipe has the answer.

It will definitely help you get hooked on spinach and enjoy all its benefits like essential minerals and protein as well as high iron content. The vitamin C in the tomatoes helps improve the absorption of iron.

Serves: 1-2
Ingredients:
- 1 cup of raw baby spinach
- 1 cup of raw zucchini, grated
- Half cup of raw cherry tomatoes, halved
- A handful of black olives, pitted and halved
- A handful of green olives, pitted and halved

Dressing Ingredients:
- 2 tablespoons of extra virgin olive oil
- Juice of 1 lime
- 2 small garlic cloves
- 1 chili flake
- Pinch of Himalaya salt
- Pinch of black pepper
- 3 segments of orange
- 3 tablespoons thick coconut milk

Delicious Vegan Salad Recipes

Instructions:
1. Start off by blending all the dressing ingredients using a blender.
2. Place the raw baby spinach onto a serving plate.
3. Top with the grated zucchini and cherry tomatoes.
4. Add the black and green olives.
5. Pour over the salsa and toss well.
6. Drizzle with the olive oil and serve.

Delicious Vegan Salad Recipes

Recipe #17 Delicious Pumpkin Surprise

The combo of pumpkin and cilantro, along with the pine nuts, and other spices, makes this salad incredibly flavorful. Adzuki beans are a great source of natural protein and vital nutrients.

Serves: 2-3
Ingredients:
- Half cup of fresh cilantro, well rinsed and dried with kitchen towel
- A handful of fresh parsley, well rinsed and dried with kitchen towel
- 1 cup of pumpkin, cooked, peeled and finely sliced
- Half cup of fresh cherry tomatoes, halved
- Half cup of adzuki beans, cooked (can be replaced by "normal" black beans)
- Half cup of raw pine nuts
- 1 teaspoon of nutmeg powder
- 1 teaspoon of curry powder
- ¼ teaspoon of Himalaya salt to taste
- 1 tablespoon of sesame seed oil

Instructions:
1. Place the fresh cilantro and parsley in a serving bowl.
2. Top with the pumpkin, adzuki or black beans, and cherry tomatoes.
3. Add the raw pine nuts and sprinkle the spices and salt over the top
4. Drizzle with the sesame seed oil and serve.
5. Enjoy!

Delicious Vegan Salad Recipes

Recipe #18 Raw Almost Green Energy Boost Salad

The combination of spinach and tomatoes as well as orange in this salad is another example of how the body's ability to absorb the high iron content of the spinach is boosted by pairing it with another vegetable that is high in vitamin C.

Turn to this salad whenever in need of natural energy.

Serves: 2-3

Ingredients:
- 1 cup fresh baby spinach leaves
- 1 raw green sweet pepper, sliced
- 1 cup raw cherry tomatoes, halved
- 1 big orange, peeled and segmented
- ¼ cup raw pistachios, roughly chopped
- 1 big ripe avocado, peeled, pitted and sliced
- 1 tablespoon extra-virgin avocado oil

Instructions:
1. Place the baby spinach in a serving bowl.
2. Top with the rest of the ingredients.
3. Add the raw pistachios.
4. Drizzle with the avocado oil, serve.

Delicious Vegan Salad Recipes

Recipe #19 Nourishing Herbal Avocado Salad

The herbs used in this salad make avocado taste amazing and they also add to the mineral and nutrient content of this salad.

Serves: 2
Ingredients:
- 2 avocados, peeled, halved and pitted
- ¼ cup of mixed Mediterranean herbs (for example thyme, rosemary, basil, oregano, parsley)
- ¼ cup of dried cherry tomatoes, quartered
- ¼ cup of cooked chickpeas or black beans
- Optional: 1 sheet of nori, cut into smaller pieces
- 1 tablespoon of extra virgin avocado oil
- Juice of half lemon
- Pinch of black pepper and Himalaya salt to taste, if needed

Instructions:
1. Place the avocado halves in a serving bowl.
2. Add the rest of the ingredients.
3. Drizzle with some avocado oil and lemon juice.
4. If needed, season with Himalaya salt and black pepper.
5. Enjoy!

Delicious Vegan Salad Recipes

Recipe #20 Chili Papaya Salad

The combination of spicy chili really compliments the sweetness of the papaya in this recipe. The cashew nuts add a really nice crunch and a hearty dose of protein.

The addition of cucumber helps stay hydrated and quench the heat of the chili. Sometimes, I like to serve this salad recipe with fresh apple and cucumber juice. Full on healing mode on!

Serves: 1
Ingredients:
- 3 tablespoons of Mediterranean herbs mix
- 1 cup of diced fresh papaya
- 4 fresh cucumbers, finely sliced
- Half teaspoon of fresh red chili powder
- A handful of raw cashew nuts, roughly chopped
- 1 tablespoon of virgin olive oil

Instructions:
1. Place herbs in a serving bowl.
2. Top with the cucumber, papaya and cashews.
3. Sprinkle the chopped chili and coconut shavings over the top and toss together.
4. Drizzle with the olive oil and serve.
5. Enjoy!

Delicious Vegan Salad Recipes

Recipe #21 Pineapple Crunchy Protein Salad

This salad is another spicy fruity option with a "multidimensional" taste. The Brazil nuts bring along some crunchy protein. This salad is perfect as a healthy brunch or a quick snack.

Serves: 2-3
Ingredients:
- Half cup of cilantro, well rinsed and dried off with kitchen towel
- 1 big pineapple, peeled and cut into smaller pieces
- Half teaspoon of red chili powder
- Half cup of raw Brazil nuts, roughly chopped
- 1 teaspoon of cinnamon powder
- 4 tablespoons of thick coconut milk

Instructions:
1. Place the fresh cilantro leaves into a serving bowl.
2. Top with the pineapple and Brazil nuts.
3. Sprinkle over the chili powder and toss together.
4. Sprinkle over the cinnamon.
5. Drizzle with the coconut milk and serve.
6. Enjoy!

Delicious Vegan Salad Recipes

Recipe #22 Arugula Pears Seduction Salad

Here is yet another example of how one can get creative with different flavor combinations while enjoying the healing nutrition of vegan salad lifestyle.

Serves: 1-2
Ingredients:
- 1 cup of fresh arugula leaves
- 2 large pears, thinly sliced
- Juice of half a lemon
- 1 tablespoon of any vegan friendly mustard
- Half cup raw pecan nuts, roughly chopped
- Half ripe avocado, sliced
- 1 tablespoon of aw seed mix
- Optional: 2 tablespoons of nutritional yeast

Instructions:
1. Place the arugula leaves into a serving bowl.
2. Top with the sliced pears and drizzle with lemon juice and vegan mustard.
3. Add the raw pecan nuts and the sliced avocado.
4. Sprinkle the raw seeds and nutritional yeast over the top of the salad and serve.

Delicious Vegan Salad Recipes

Recipe #23 Iceberg Hydration Salad

Lettuce has a high-water content and it blends really well with the cucumber. This salad is designed to help you maintain hydration throughout a long hot day while keeping your belly and taste buds satisfied.

Serves: 2-3
Ingredients:
- 1 small iceberg lettuce, washed, dried and chopped
- 4 raw carrots, peeled and thinly sliced, or spiralized
- 4 raw cucumbers, peeled and sliced
- 3 chili flakes, cut into micro pieces (you can also use half teaspoon of chili powder)
- Half cup of raw pistachios, roughly chopped
- Optional: 2 nori sheets, cut or torn into smaller pieces
- 1 tablespoon of sesame seed oil

Instructions:
1. Mix all the ingredients in a big salad bowl.
2. Drizzle with sesame seed oil and if needed season with Himalaya salt and black pepper.
3. Enjoy!

Recipe #24 Oriental Creamy Iceberg Dream

Fresh iceberg lettuce combines really well with creamy ingredients such as cashews, avocado and coconut oil.
It's a very simple and refreshing green salad recipe that is beginner friendly. It's also a fantastic side dish.

Serves: 2-3
Ingredients:
- 1 small iceberg lettuce, washed, dried and chopped
- 1 big ripe avocado, peeled, pitted and sliced
- 6 tablespoons of thick coconut milk
- Half cup of raw, unsalted cashew nuts
- 4 tablespoons chopped chives
- Pinch of black pepper, Himalaya salt and chili powder to taste

Instructions:
1. In a medium sized salad bowl, combine the lettuce, avocado slices, cashews and chives.
2. Mix well.
3. Now, drizzle with coconut milk and sprinkle some black pepper, Himalaya salt and chili powder to taste if needed.
4. Toss well, serve and enjoy!

Delicious Vegan Salad Recipes

Recipe #25 Green Protein Salad

This salad is pure health. It combines chlorophyll rich kale that is also a great source of vegan protein with other protein-packed plant-based ingredients.

This recipe is just perfect as a take away lunch.

Serves: 2
Ingredients:
- 1 cup of fresh kale leaves, washed and chopped, stems removed
- Half cup of raw green beans, julienned
- Half cup of mung bean sprouts
- Half cup of raw hazel nuts, roughly chopped
- 3 nori sheets, cut or torn into smaller pieces
- 2 tablespoons of olive oil
- Juice of half lime or lemon
- Optional: Himalaya salt and black pepper to taste
- A few orange wedges, to serve

Instructions:
1. Combine all the ingredients in a medium sized salad bowl.
2. Sprinkle over some olive oil and fresh lemon or lime juice.
3. Toss well.
4. Serve with a few orange wedges.
5. Enjoy!

Delicious Vegan Salad Recipes

Recipe #26 Sweet Pepper Dream

This simple to follow salad recipe, proves once again how a vegan salad lifestyle can be both interesting and nutritious.

Serves: 2-4
Ingredients:
- 1 cup of spinach leaves, washed, dried and chopped
- Half cup of small cherry tomatoes, halved
- 1 red sweet pepper, sliced
- 1 yellow sweet pepper, sliced
- 1 orange sweet pepper, sliced
- 1 cup of black olives, pitted and halved
- Half cup of cooked chickpeas
- 2 tablespoons of extra virgin olive oil
- Juice of 1 lemon
- Optional: Himalaya salt to season

Instructions:
1. Place all the salad ingredients in a big salad bowl.
2. Toss well.
3. Drizzle with olive oil and lemon juice.
4. Season with Himalaya salt if needed and toss again.
5. Enjoy!

Delicious Vegan Salad Recipes

Recipe #27 Creamy Spinach Strawberry Salad

The strawberries are high in anti-oxidants which help the body to absorb the abundance of iron that is provided by the raw spinach. Coconut milk and avocado, mixed with nutmeg, ginger and cinnamon make this salad incredibly creamy while adding to anti-inflammatory properties and naturally sweet taste. Cashews are also in the "Creamy Club" and they bring some natural protein to the table.

Serves: 2
Ingredients:
- 1 cup of baby spinach leaves
- 1 cup of fresh strawberries, halved
- Half cup of raw, unsalted cashews

For the Dressing:
- Half of a ripe avocado, peeled and pitted
- Half cup of thick coconut milk
- Half teaspoon of powder
- Half teaspoon of nutmeg powder
- Half teaspoon of ginger powder

Instructions:
1. In a medium sized salad bowl, combine the spinach, strawberries and cashews.
2. Mix well.
3. Using a blender, blend avocado, coconut milk, cinnamon, nutmeg and ginger. Process until smooth.
4. Now, combine the creamy blend with the salad. Enjoy!

Delicious Vegan Salad Recipes

Recipe #28 Easy Red Cabbage Grape Salad

Red cabbage is very high in dietary fiber, making this recipe another energy sustaining option to keep you going all afternoon. This is also another example of how "outside the box" your vegan salads can be.

Serves: 1-2
Ingredients:
- Half cup of raw red cabbage, shredded
- 4 small raw carrots, peeled and grated
- Half cup of red grapes, halved
- Half cup of raw cashews, roughly chopped
- 1 ripe avocado, pitted and sliced
- 2 tablespoons of thick cashew milk
- Fresh juice of 1 lime

Instructions:
1. Place all the ingredients in a medium-sized salad bowl.
2. Drizzle with cashew milk and lime juice.
3. Toss well, serve and enjoy!

Delicious Vegan Salad Recipes

Recipe #29 Tasty Dinner Vegan Ratatouille

This recipe is one of my favorite dinner recipes, but it could also be served as lunch.

It's jam packed with vitamins, minerals and natural protein and super easy to make.

As you may have noticed by now, I am a big fan of Nori. While most people associate it only with sushi, it's actually a really nice salad ingredient and adds in even more vital nutrients to stimulate massive healing.

Serves: 1-2
Ingredients:
- 1 cup of fresh cherry tomatoes, halved
- 1 cup of raw, or slightly cooked zucchini, thinly sliced
- 1 small red onion, finely chopped
- 1 clove of fresh garlic, finely chopped
- 2 nori sheets, torn or cut into smaller pieces
- A handful of fresh basil leaves, finely chopped
- 1 cup of black olives, pitted and halved
- A handful of raw pine nuts
- 2 tablespoons of extra virgin olive oil
- 2 tablespoons of fresh tomatoe juice
- Optional: Himalaya salt and black pepper to taste.

Instructions:
1. Place the cherry tomatoes in to a serving bowl.
2. Add the chopped onion, garlic and fresh basil.

Delicious Vegan Salad Recipes

3. Add the black olives, nuts and nori.
4. Drizzle over the olive oil and tomato juice.
5. Toss together. Season with black pepper and Himalaya salt if needed. Enjoy!

Delicious Vegan Salad Recipes

Recipe #30 Quinoa Curry Salad

You don't have to cook for hours to enjoy a good curry dish. This recipe proves just that.

You can easily use some quinoa leftovers and mix it with other ingredients such as cashew nuts to get a solid protein source as well as healthy fats.

Serves: 2-3
Ingredients:
- 2 cups of cooked quinoa
- Half cup of raw cashew nuts, roughly chopped
- 2 green bell peppers, sliced
- A handful of arugula leaves
- 1 teaspoon of fresh red chili, seeded and finely chopped
- 1 teaspoon of fresh turmeric root, finely chopped
- 1 teaspoon of fresh garlic, finely chopped
- 1 teaspoon of fresh coriander, finely chopped
- 1 teaspoon of fresh curry powder
- 4 tablespoons of thick coconut milk

Instructions:
1. Place all the ingredients in a salad bowl.
2. Add in the spices and coconut milk.
3. Toss well.
4. If needed, season with Himalaya salt and black pepper.
5. Enjoy!

Delicious Vegan Salad Recipes

Recipe #31 Comfort Sweet Potato Salad

This is another easy to make, comforting recipe that is just perfect for dinner. Oh, and leftovers make a great takeaway lunch. The combination of high fiber foods in this recipe makes it another great option when choosing what to have for dinner as it will be slowly digested without weighing you down.

Serves: 2-3
Ingredients:
- 1 cup of sweet potato, peeled, cooked and cut into smaller pieces
- 1 cup of red cabbage, shredded
- 1 cup of cherry tomatoes, halved
- Handful of cashew nuts, roughly chopped
- 1 small onion, finely chopped
- 1 teaspoon of fresh basil leaves, finely chopped
- Half cup of black olives, pitted and finely chopped
- Juice of half a lemon
- 4 tablespoons of vegan mayonnaise
- 4 tablespoons of raw pumpkin seeds
- Pinch of Himalaya salt and black pepper to season

Instructions:
1. Place the sweet potato, red cabbage, cherry tomatoes, cashews, basil, onion and olives in a salad bowl.
2. Add the mayonnaise and lemon juice while mixing well.
3. Season with Himalaya salt and black pepper.
4. Enjoy!

Delicious Vegan Salad Recipes

Recipe #32 Easy Tomato Salad

Many of my friends who think about transitioning to a plant-based way of eating, similar to mine, very often say "Oh but it will be so hard to find all the ingredients".

Well, this recipe (plus many others from this book) can easily prove them wrong.

It's all about creativity and resourcefulness. If you want to follow a healthy, vegan diet rich in salads, you will find the way, you will make the way. Especially with this easy to follow recipe!

Serves: 2
Ingredients:
- 4 large tomatoes, sliced
- 1 cup of lentils of your choice, cooked and chilled
- Half cup of black olives, pitted and roughly chopped
- 1 teaspoon of fresh garlic, finely chopped
- 1 teaspoon of fresh basil leaves, finely chopped
- 2 tablespoons of extra virgin olive oil
- Handful of fresh cilantro leaves
- Himalaya salt to taste, if needed

Instructions:
1. Place all the ingredients in a medium-sized salad bowl.
2. Drizzle with olive oil and season with Himalaya salt if needed.
3. Garnish with fresh cilantro leaves.
4. Enjoy!

Delicious Vegan Salad Recipes

Recipe #33 Avocado's Walnut Mix

Avocados are incredibly nutritious, and their high potassium and healthy fat content make them a great base for a wholesome meal. The walnuts provide a healthy dose of essential minerals and are a great source of protein.

Apple cider vinegar brings some powerful anti-oxidant properties to the table.

I love this recipe as a quick energy boost snack, or on the go lunch or dinner.

Serves: 2
Ingredients:
- 1 big ripe avocado, pitted and sliced
- 1 small red apple, cored and finely chopped
- Half cup of raw walnuts, roughly chopped
- 2 tablespoons of organic Apple Cider Vinegar
- A handful of raisins

Instructions:
1. In a bowl mix together the apples, walnuts and avocado oil.
2. Sprinkle the raisins over the top.
3. Drizzle with Apple Cider Vinegar.
4. Serve and enjoy!

Delicious Vegan Salad Recipes

Recipe #34 Avocado Strawberries Salad

This recipe shows the versatility of the avocado. It also shows how well it can blend with both sweet ingredients like strawberries with the mustardy flavor of the rocket (arugula).

It's also a fantastic way to sneak in more greens into your diet.

Serves: 1-2
Ingredients:
- 1 big ripe avocado, pitted and sliced
- 1 cup of fresh strawberries, quartered
- Half cup of raw pecan nuts, roughly chopped
- Half cup of fresh rocket (arugula) leaves, finely chopped
- 2 tablespoons of thick coconut milk
- 1 tablespoon of raw seed mix
- 1 tablespoon of coconut shavings

Instructions:
1. In a bowl, combine the strawberries, avocado, pecan nuts, fresh rocket (arugula), raw seed mix and the coconut milk.
2. Toss together.
3. Sprinkle over the coconut shavings and serve.
4. Enjoy!

Recipe #35 Aromatic Soy Sprouts Salads

This recipe is very refreshing and perfect as a quick healthy snack or a side dish.

Serves: 2-3
Ingredients:
- Two large tomatoes, quartered, skin removed
- 1 big avocado, peeled, pitted and sliced
- Half cup mixed micro herbs
- Half cup fresh soy sprouts
- Half cup raw pistachios, roughly chopped
- 2 tablespoons of organic apple cider vinegar
- Pinch of black pepper and Himalayan salt to taste if needed

Instructions:
1. Combine all the ingredients in a salad bowl.
2. Drizzle over a little apple cider vinegar and toss well.
3. If needed, season with Himalaya salt and black pepper.
4. Enjoy!

Delicious Vegan Salad Recipes

Recipe #36 Stuffed Zucchini Salad

While zucchini in itself can be a bit boring, herbs can really spice it up and almost turn it into a different vegetable.

Serves: 2
Ingredients:
- 2 large raw zucchinis
- Half cup of mixed Mediterranean herbs (like oregano, thyme, rosemary)
- Half cup of raw pine nuts
- 1 small avocado, diced
- 2 tablespoons of olive oil or avocado oil
- 1 tablespoon of raw seed mix

Instructions:
1. Cut the zucchinis in half and scoop out the flesh using a teaspoon.
2. Chop the zucchini flesh and place it in a bowl.
3. To the bowl that contains the zucchini flesh, add the herbs, pine nuts and avocado.
4. Toss together with the olive oil.
5. Place the zucchini shells on a serving plate.
6. Stuff the zucchini shells with the micro herb mixture.
7. Sprinkle the raw seed mix over the top.
8. Drizzle over a little extra virgin olive oil and serve.

Delicious Vegan Salad Recipes

Recipe #37 Natural Detox Recipe

Ginger is great for digestive problems and acts as a natural anti-inflammatory. This recipe is a great option if you want to restore your energy levels and improve your digestion.

Serves: 2
Ingredients:
- 4 large carrots, peeled and chopped
- Juice of 1 orange
- 1 mango, peeled, pitted and chopped
- 2 inch of ginger
- 1 big onion, minced
- 1 red bell pepper, sliced
- 2 garlic cloves, peeled and minced
- Half cup cilantro, chopped
- Handful of sunflower seeds
- Himalayan/sea salt to taste

Instructions:
1. Place all the ingredients in a big salad bowl.
2. Add a pinch of Himalayan salt to taste. Sprinkle some fresh orange juice, cilantro and sunflower seeds over the soup.
3. Enjoy!

Delicious Vegan Salad Recipes

Recipe #38 Spicy Exotic Salad

This salad is quick and easy to prepare and a fantastic way of eating especially in the summer.

Serves: 3
Ingredients:
- 1/4 cup cilantro
- Half cup spinach leaves
- 1 zucchini
- 2 nori sheets, cut or torn into smaller pieces
- 2 garlic cloves, peeled
- Half cup of radish
- Half cup of raw cashews
- Half teaspoon of turmeric powder
- Pinch of black pepper (real game changer as it helps your body get all the anti-inflammatory benefits that turmeric powder offers)
- Pinch of Himalayan salt
- 1 tablespoon avocado oil

Instructions:
1. Combine all the ingredients in a salad bowl.
2. Squeeze some fresh lime or lemon juice into the mixture, and enjoy!
3. Serve and enjoy.

Delicious Vegan Salad Recipes

Recipe #39 Spicy Raw Veggie Noodles

If you don't have a spiralizer, you can still enjoy the healing benefits of this salad. Simply turn the veggies into very thin slices.

Serves: 2
Ingredients:
- 4 carrots, peeled and spiralized
- 2 zucchinis, peeled and spiralized
- 1 tablespoon of coconut oil
- A handful of fresh cilantro leaves
- Half cup of dried fruit of your choice (for example raisins)
- 2 tablespoons of Apple cider vinegar or lemon juice
- Himalaya salt to taste
- Half teaspoon of curry powder
- Half teaspoon of chili powder

Instructions:
1. First, stir-fry the spiralized zucchini and carrots in coconut oil, curry and chili powder using low heat.
2. Turn off the heat after a few minutes (which is enough for the spiralized veggies to absorb the coconut oil and spices).
3. Place the spiralized veggies in a salad bowl.
4. Add cilantro leaves and dried fruit of your choice.
5. Drizzle with apple cider vinegar or lemon juice.
6. Season with some Himalaya salt.
7. Enjoy!

Delicious Vegan Salad Recipes

Recipe #40 Summer Salsa Salad

When you have a look at this salad, it's not particularly the salad ingredients that draw attention. It's the salsa! In fact, it's so good, that it can make any veggie taste great.

Serves: 2-3
Ingredients:
- 1 red organic beetroot, peeled and sliced
- 6 whole radishes, sliced
- 2 small zucchinis, sliced and steamed to soften up
- 2 red peppers, deseeded and sliced
- Half cup of soy sprouts
- 1 green apple, peeled, diced and sliced

Dressing:
- 2 tablespoons of olive oil (extra virgin)
- 2 teaspoons of fresh oregano, chopped
- 1 clove of garlic, peeled and finely chopped
- 1 teaspoon of organic maple syrup
- 1 tablespoon of fresh parsley leaves, chopped
- Fresh juice of 1 lemon
- Himalayan salt to taste

Instructions:
1. To make the dressing, whisk some olive oil with 1 clove of chopped garlic and maple syrup.
2. Add lemon juice, sea salt, parsley, and oregano.
3. Whisk again to combine.
4. Set aside in a fridge while you are preparing the salad.
5. Mix the sliced veggies in a big bowl.

Delicious Vegan Salad Recipes

6. Add the apple.
7. Drizzle the salad dressing on top to serve the salad.

Delicious Vegan Salad Recipes

Recipe #41 Spice It Up Papaya Salad

Green papaya combines really well with carrots and arugula. But the "secret sauce" is the Chili Spicy Dressing.

Ingredients:
- 1 small green papaya, julienned
- Half cup of arugula leaves
- Half cup of cooked basmati rice
- 2 carrots, peeled and spiralized (or sliced thinly)
- 1 big avocado, peeled, pitted and sliced
- One small red onion, sliced
- A handful of raisins

For the Chili Spicy Dressing:
- 1 tablespoon of raw coconut vinegar
- 1 tablespoon of cane sugar or maple syrup
- 1 red long chili, seeded and finely chopped
- Juice of 2 limes
- 1 small clove of garlic, peeled and minced

Instructions:
1. Whisk all the dressing ingredients in a small bowl. Set aside in a fridge to cool.
2. In the meantime, prepare the salad by tossing all the salad ingredients together in a salad bowl.
3. Add the rice and toss well.
4. Now mix the salad with the dressing so that all ingredients are equally covered.
5. Enjoy!

Delicious Vegan Salad Recipes

Recipe #42 Easy Chia Snack Salad

This recipe is packed with natural protein and good fats. Oh and it's so easy to make and tastes delicious. Great as a natural, after-dinner treat or a quick snack during the day!

Serves: 2-4

Ingredients:
For the Salad:
- Half cup of blueberries
- Half cup of strawberries, halved
- Half avocado, peeled and diced

For the Salsa:
- 8 tablespoons chia seeds or chia seed powder
- Half teaspoon of vanilla powder
- Half teaspoon of cinnamon
- 1 tablespoon of maple syrup
- Half cup of thick coconut milk

Instructions:
1. Place the blueberries, strawberries and avocado in a salad bowl.
2. In a separate bowl, combine all the salsa ingredients. Whisk well.
3. Now, pour the salsa over the fruit salad.
4. Place in a fridge for a few hours.
5. Serve chilled.
6. Enjoy!

Delicious Vegan Salad Recipes

Recipe #43 Tantalizing Thai Salad

This salad will make anyone crave more and more veggies.

Green apples combine really well with the spicy sauce. It's also a fantastic way to combine raw food with cooked food.

Serves: 2-3
Ingredients:
- 4 carrots, peeled and spiralized or thinly sliced
- Half cup of green onions (shallots), finely chopped
- 2 green bell peppers, sliced
- 1 cup of finely chopped red cabbage
- 2 green apples, peeled and sliced
- 1 cup of broccoli, cooked and cut into small pieces
- 1 cup of cooked basmati rice and beans to serve

Sauce:
- 4 dates soaked in warm water for about thirty minutes
- Handful of raw cashews
- 2 tablespoons of agave nectar
- 2 tablespoons of tamari (soy sauce)
- Juice of one lime
- 1 teaspoon of red chili pepper

Instructions:
1. Place all the salad ingredients in a salad bowl.
2. Blend all the sauce ingredients using a blender or a food processor.
3. Pour the salsa over the salad and serve with some basmati rice and beans.

Delicious Vegan Salad Recipes

Recipe #44 Carrot & Cucumber in Spicy Green Salsa

This recipe is incredibly nutritious as aside from beautiful, raw fruits and veggies, it also uses spirulina powder. Spirulina is a very helpful natural supplement and energy balancer for vegans as it's a great natural source of iron and protein.

Serves: 2
Ingredients:
For the Salad:
- 4 big raw cucumbers, peeled and sliced
- 6 carrots, peeled, spiralized
- 1 cup of greens of your choice (I like kale or arugula)
- Half lime

For the Dressing:
- 1 medium sized avocado, peeled and pitted
- 1 big orange, peeled and cut into smaller pieces
- 2 big garlic cloves, peeled
- 1 teaspoon spirulina powder
- Pinch of Himalaya salt
- 1 small chili flake

Instructions:
1. Place all the salad ingredients in a salad bowl.
2. Drizzle with fresh lime juice and set aside.
3. Proceed to making the salad dressing by blending all the dressing ingredients in a blender or food processor.
4. Now, combine the dressing with the salad, toss well, serve and enjoy!

Delicious Vegan Salad Recipes

Recipe #45 Easy Ginger Almond Salad

Ginger is an amazing addition to this healing, raw alkaline vegan recipe.

Serves: 2
Ingredients:
- 2-inch piece of fresh ginger, peeled and sliced
- 1 clove of garlic, peeled and chopped
- Handful of raw cashews, crushed
- Handful of fresh parsley
- Handful of arugula leaves
- 2 green apples, sliced and diced
- 2 cucumbers, peeled and sliced
- Pinch of cinnamon
- Half lime
- 1 tablespoon of organic apple cider vinegar
- Optional: Himalaya salt to taste

Instructions:
1. Place all the ingredients in a salad bowl.
2. Drizzle with fresh lime juice and apple cider vinegar.
3. Toss well, serve and enjoy!

Delicious Vegan Salad Recipes

Recipe #46 Beautiful Skin Salad with a Coconut Dressing

This salad combines the best beta-carotene rich fruits and veggies to help you have healthy looking skin. It's also very rich in vitamin A to help you protect your eye sight.

Serves: 2
Ingredients:
- 2 big tomatoes, sliced
- 2 big carrots, peeled and sliced
- 2 beets, sliced
- Half cup of soaked almonds
- 4 mandarins, peeled and segmented
- A handful of fresh parsley
- 2 tablespoons of apple cider vinegar

Instructions:
1. Place all the ingredients in a salad bowl.
2. Drizzle with apple cider vinegar.
3. Serve and enjoy!

Extra tip from Karen: this recipe can also be turned into a smoothie or a soup. Simply place all the salad ingredients through a blender and add some filtered water or any plant-based milk of your choice.

Instead of water or vegan milk, you could also use some fresh tomatoes or carrot juice for optimal benefits.

Delicious Vegan Salad Recipes

Recipe #47 Spicy Pepper Salad

This salad is very rich in protein and iron. Vitamin C helps boost the immune system while providing you with more energy, naturally. For optimal benefits and nutrition, serve this salad with a spirulina maca smoothie. (recipe below the main salad recipe). Enjoy!

Serves: 2
Ingredients:
- 2 yellow bell peppers, diced and sliced
- 1 cup of lentils, cooked
- Half cup of baby spinach
- 1 orange, peeled and cut into smaller pieces
- 2 big sweet potatoes, peeled and cooked

For the salad dressing:
- 1 teaspoon of curry powder
- 1 teaspoon of sweet paprika powder
- 2 tablespoons of lime juice
- 1 tablespoon of olive or avocado oil
- 2 tablespoons of thick coconut milk
- Sea salt to taste (optional)

Instructions:
1. Combine all the salad ingredients in a big salad bowl.
2. Now, combine the dressing ingredients and whisk well.
3. Pour the dressing over the salad, toss well and enjoy!

Delicious Vegan Salad Recipes

Bonus Recipe:

Spirulina Maca Antioxidant Smoothie

-Blend a handful of blueberries with 1 cup of coconut milk, half teaspoon maca powder and 1 teaspoon spirulina powder.

Serve with the salad.
Enjoy!

Delicious Vegan Salad Recipes

Recipe #48 Recycle Salad with Vegan Coconut Yoghurt Dip

Do you have any fruit leftovers in your fridge?

If so, use them to make this delicious salad.

Serves: 2
Ingredients:
- 2 cups of any fruit of your choice
- Half cup of any nuts and seeds of your choice
- A handful of fresh mint leaves to garnish

Ingredients to make the vegan yoghurt dressing:
- 1 cup of vegan coconut yogurt (or other vegan yoghurt of your choice)
- 1 teaspoon of vanilla essence
- 1 teaspoon of ground cinnamon
- 1 teaspoon of raw cocoa powder
- 1 tablespoon of desiccated coconut
- 1 tablespoon of ginger powder

Instructions:
1. Combine the fruit in a salad bowl.
2. In a separate bowl, mix all the vegan yoghurt dressing ingredients.
3. Pour the dressing over the salad.
4. Mix well, garnish with some fresh mint leaves and enjoy!

Delicious Vegan Salad Recipes

Recipe #49 Fresh Basil Potato Salad

There is just something amazing about the flavor combination of tomato and basil. And there is definitely something amazing about the flavor combination of potatoes and mayonnaise.

This salad is very tasty, filling and nutritious.

Serves: 2-3
Ingredients:
- Half cup of fresh basil leaves
- Half cup of cherry tomatoes, halved
- 1 tablespoon of raw pine nuts
- 4 big potatoes, peeled, sliced, cooked and cooled down
- 4 tablespoons of vegan mayonnaise
- Pinch of Himalaya salt and black pepper to taste

Instructions:
1. In a medium sized salad bowl, place the fresh basil leaves and add the halved cherry tomatoes.
2. Add the potatoes and top with the raw pine nuts.
3. Combine with vegan mayonnaise and toss well.
4. Salt and pepper can be added to taste.
5. Enjoy!

Delicious Vegan Salad Recipes

Recipe #50 Detox Pomegranate 3 Ingredient Salad

This is a very refreshing and easy to make, detoxifying salad. Perfect if you want to revitalize your body and mind.

Serves: 2-3
Ingredients for the salad:
- 1 cup of raw red cabbage, shredded
- Half cup cucumber slices
- Half cup pomegranate seeds

Ingredients for the dressing:
- Juice of half lime
- 2 tablespoons of coconut milk
- Pinch of ginger powder
- Pinch of nutmeg powder

Instructions:
1. Combine all the salad ingredients.
2. In a separate bowl, whisk all the dressing ingredients together.
3. Pour over the salad.
4. Serve and enjoy!

Delicious Vegan Salad Recipes

Recipe #51 Quick Quinoa Salad

Quinoa is a gluten-free, easy to digest grain that is just perfect for salads. It's rich in protein and combines well with all kinds of tastes, sweet, savory and spicy.

I always have some cooked quinoa at hand to add to my salads.

Serves: 2-3

Ingredients:

- 1 cup of cooked quinoa
- ¼ cup of cherry tomatoes, halved
- ¼ cup of raw almonds, chopped
- 1 small and ripe avocado (peeled and diced)
- ¼ cup of arugula leaves
- 2 tablespoons of vegan mustard
- 1 medium-sized endive, sliced
- Half lemon, juiced
- Himalaya salt and black pepper to taste

Instructions:

1. Place all the salad ingredients into a salad. Mix well.
2. Add a bit of vegan mustard and lemon juice and stir well.
3. If needed, season with Himalayan salt and black pepper.
4. Toss well to combine.
5. Enjoy!

Delicious Vegan Salad Recipes

Recipe #52 Arugula Lentil Salad with Lemon Parsley Dressing

This salad's dressing is incredibly nutritious as it combines parsley with lemon. It tastes great too!

Serves: 2
Ingredients:

- 1 cup of cooked red lentils, cooled down
- 1 cup of fresh arugula, chopped
- 1 ripe avocado, peeled, pitted, and cubed
- Lime or lemon wedges to garnish

For the dressing:

- 2 tablespoons of extra virgin olive oil
- 6 tablespoons of parsley, chopped
- 2 tablespoons of coconut milk
- A pinch of pepper and Himalaya salt
- 1 big garlic clove, peeled

Instructions:

1. Place all the salad ingredients in a salad bowl. Mix well.
2. In a blender, or a small hand blender, combine all the dressing ingredients until smooth.
3. Pour the dressing into the salad bowl and toss well. Garnish with some lime or lemon wedges. Enjoy!

Delicious Vegan Salad Recipes

Recipe #53 Black Beans & Olive Salad

This salad is great as quick dinner or take away lunch. It's packed with protein and good carbs.

Serves: 1-2
Ingredients:

- Half cup of black beans, cooked
- Half cup of black olives, pitted
- 2 whole medium sweet potatoes (boiled and cooled)
- A few onion rings
- Handful of fresh parsley
- Himalaya salt to taste
- Juice of half lime
- 1 tablespoon of organic olive or avocado oil

Instructions:

1. Place all the salad ingredients in a salad bowl.

2. Drizzle with fresh lime juice and avocado or olive oil.

3. Season with Himalaya salt if needed, enjoy!

Delicious Vegan Salad Recipes

Recipe #54 Roasted Broccoli Salad

This salad offers a unique mix of roasted broccoli and adzuki beans. It's a nice, warm salad, perfect for a busy winter day.

You can find adzuki beans in your local health store, or order it from Amazon.

Servings: 1-2
Ingredients:

- 1 cup of broccoli, chopped and cooked (still warm)
- Half cup of cooked adzuki beans (still warm)
- 2 tablespoons of coconut oil
- Half teaspoon of curry powder
- A pinch of sea salt
- Black pepper and chili powder, to taste

Instructions:

1. In a salad bowl, combine the cooked broccoli and adzuki beans.
2. Spread over the coconut oil until melted.
3. Season with curry powder, sea salt, black pepper and chili.
4. Toss well and enjoy!

Delicious Vegan Salad Recipes

Recipe #55 Smoked Tofu and Sweet Potato Green Salad

Smoked tofu, fresh greens and cooked potatoes with fresh herbs, spices and (optional) some vegan mayo is an amazing take away lunch or a quick on the go meal.

Serves: 1-2
Ingredients:

- Half cup of smoked tofu, cut into smaller pieces
- 2 large sweet potatoes, cooked, diced, and cooled down
- 1 tablespoon of vegan mayo (optional)
- 2 large tomato, sliced
- 1 cup of fresh watercress
- 1 tablespoon of apple cider vinegar
- A dash of ground black pepper and Himalayan salt

Instructions:

1. Place all the ingredients into a salad bowl. Stir well.
2. Add the vegan mayo, apple cider vinegar, pepper and salt.
3. Toss well, serve and enjoy!

Recipe #56 Easy Artichoke Detox Salad

Artichokes are highly alkalizing and full of magnesium and potassium.

They're just perfect for a healing, refreshing green salad like this one!

Serves: 1-2
Ingredients:

- 1 cup of canned artichoke hearts, halved
- 1 cup of fresh baby spinach
- Half cup of radish, halved
- Half of red onion, sliced
- 2 tablespoons of lime juice or apple cider vinegar
- Pinch of Himalayan salt to taste

Instructions:

1. Mix all of the salad ingredients in a large bowl.
2. Stir well while adding the lime juice or apple cider vinegar.
3. Season with Himalayan salt.
4. Serve and enjoy!

Delicious Vegan Salad Recipes

Recipe #57 No More Sugar Cravings Salad

This salad is great for a quick snack! It's full of good fats to help you reduce sugar cravings.

Serves: 1
Ingredients:

- 4 tablespoons of cooked quinoa
- 1 whole avocado, peeled, pitted and sliced
- 1 tablespoon of melted coconut oil
- Handful of fresh cilantro
- A pinch of sea salt to taste and Himalaya salt to taste

Instructions:

1. Place all the ingredients in a salad bowl and stir well.
2. Pour over some melted coconut oil.
3. Season with Himalaya salt and black pepper.

Delicious Vegan Salad Recipes

Recipe #58 Easy Quinoa Salad

This salad combines the anti-inflammatory benefits of curry while sneaking in some nutrient-packed greens. Raisins and grapes make this salad taste irresistible.

Serves: 1-2

Ingredients:

- Half cup of cooked quinoa
- 1 cup of red grapes, halved
- Handful of raisins
- Handful of raw walnuts
- 1 small red onion, peeled and chopped
- 2 tablespoons of vegan mustard
- 1 cup of mixed baby greens
- Half teaspoon of curry powder
- Half teaspoon of black pepper
- Himalayan salt to season

Instructions:

1. Place all the ingredients in a salad bowl and stir well.
2. Season with some Himalayan salt if needed.
3. You can serve it right away or serve in the fridge for later.
4. Enjoy!

Bonus Recipes

Bonus Recipes

This chapter contains bonus recipes that you can add to your healthy vegan salads or serve along.

Enjoy!

Bonus Recipes

Recipe #1 Comfort Wellness Smoothie

This recipe uses hemp oil which is a highly therapeutic oil to re-balance hormones, soothe anxiety and enhance the mood.

Serves 1-2
Ingredients:

- 1 big sweet potato, peeled and cooked
- 1 tablespoon of hemp oil
- 1 cup of coconut milk
- Half an avocado, pitted and peeled
- A handful of fresh mint leaves
- Pinch of Himalayan salt
- Pinch of maca powder and cinnamon powder

Instructions:

1. Place all the ingredients in a blender.
2. Process until smooth.
3. Serve in a smoothie glass, or a bowl and enjoy!

Bonus Recipes

Recipe #2 Digestive Smoothie

This smoothie is great for digestion and relaxation. It can also be used as a salad dressing for fruit salads.

Serves 1-2
Ingredients:

- 1 teaspoon of fresh mint leaves
- 1 green apple, peeled and diced
- Half cup of almond milk
- Half teaspoon of fresh vanilla
- Half cup fennel infusion, cooled

Instructions:

1. Place all the ingredients in a blender.
2. Process until smooth.
3. Pour into a smoothie glass, serve and enjoy!

Bonus Recipes

Recipe #3 Beauty Balance Smoothie

Good fats from avocado and coconut oil will help you stay full longer and prevent sugar cravings.

At the same time the high beta-carotene content will help you have a glowing, healthy looking skin. This smoothie can also be a salad dressing for any leafy green or veggie salad.

Serves 1-2
Ingredients:

- 1 cup of cashew or coconut milk
- 4 small carrots, peeled and chopped
- 4 fresh tomatoes, washed and peeled
- Handful of fresh parsley, washed
- 1 teaspoon of moringa powder
- Himalaya salt to taste

Instructions:

1. Place all the ingredients in a blender.
2. Process until smooth.
3. Pour into a smoothie glass, stir well, serve and enjoy!

Bonus Recipes

Recipe #4 Protein Smoothie

This smoothie can be also served as a nice soup (warm or cold) or as a salad dressing for any veggie or leafy green salad of your choice.

Serves: 2-3
Ingredients:

- 1 cup of organic peas
- 4 carrots, peeled and chopped
- A handful of fresh cilantro
- 1 cup coconut or almond milk, unsweetened
- Himalayan salt and black pepper to taste

Instructions:

1. Place all the ingredients in a blender.
2. Process until smooth.
3. Serve in a smoothie glass or a bowl.

Enjoy cold or slightly warm.

Bonus Recipes

Recipe #5 Flaxseed Protein Smoothie

The flaxseed meal is an excellent source of Omega-3 fatty acids, aka "good fats".

Perfect healthy vegan smoothie and it can also supplement your salads or be used as a salad dip for veggie salads and leafy green salads.

Serves: 1-2
Ingredients:

- 1 big avocado, peeled and pitted
- 1 cup of coconut milk
- 1 lime, peeled
- Pinch of Himalaya salt
- 2 teaspoons of flaxseed meal
- A handful of fresh baby spinach, washed
- 1 teaspoon of fresh moringa powder

Instructions:

1. Place all ingredients in a blender.
2. Blend until combined and almonds are blitzed.
3. Serve into a chilled glass and enjoy!

Bonus Recipes

Recipe #6 Homemade Trail Mix

By mixing your own trail mix, using organic, raw ingredients you are ensuring that you get a healthy, energy-boosting snack that you can trust.

This mix is perfect to add to your salads, or smoothies to make a healthy and nutritious smoothie bowl.

Makes approximately 4 ¼ Cup

Ingredients:

- 4 tablespoons of raw cashew nuts, whole
- 4 tablespoons of raw brazil nuts, whole
- 4 tablespoons of raw seed mix
- 4 tablespoons of dried berry mix
- 4 tablespoons of coconut flakes
- 4 tablespoons of raw cocoa nibs
- 4 tablespoons of dried mango pieces
- 4 tablespoons of dried apple pieces

Instructions:

Place all the ingredients into a large mixing bowl and toss together well. Store in a jar.

Bonus Recipes

Recipe #7 Green Nutrition Smoothie

This recipe can be both a smoothie as well as salad dressing or a nutritious dip.

Oh...and it could also be served as a raw or slightly cooked soup. The simplicity of a balanced vegan diet never ceases to amaze me.

Serves 1-2
Ingredients:

- 1 tablespoon of olive oil
- 1 cup of coconut milk, unsweetened
- Half cup of broccoli, cooked
- Half cup of artichoke hearts, cooked
- Half cup of kale
- Half cup of arugula
- 1 green apple, peeled and sliced
- Dash of salt

Instructions:

1. Combine all the ingredients in a blender.
2. Process until smooth.
3. Serve and enjoy!

Bonus Recipes

Recipe #8 Soothing Lavender Pegan Smoothie

This smoothie can also be used as a salad dressing, especially for fruit salads, melon salads and papaya salads.

Serves 1-2
Ingredients:
- 1 teaspoon of culinary lavender
- 1 cup of coconut water
- 2 sprigs of mint
- 1 avocado, peeled and pitted
- 1 cup of strawberries or blueberries
- 1 teaspoon of spirulina
- 1 teaspoon of maple syrup
- Half teaspoon of cinnamon powder
- ¼ teaspoon Ashwagandha powder

Instructions:
1. Place all the ingredients in a blender.
2. Process well until smooth and enjoy your smoothie.
3. Place the leftovers in the fridge to use as a sweet salad dressing.
4. Enjoy!

Bonus Recipes

Recipe #9 Nutritious Vanilla Smoothie

This is another naturally sweet green smoothie, that is packed with nutrients. You can use it as a salad dressing for any sweet fruit salad.

Serves:1-2
Ingredients:

- 1 natural vanilla bean
- 1 cup of cashew milk
- 1 banana, peeled
- 2 tablespoons of nutritional yeast
- Half cup of kale leaves

Instructions:

1. Place all the ingredients in a blender.
2. Process until smooth.
3. Serve and enjoy as a smoothie or salad dressing for any sweet fruity salad recipe of your choice.
4. It will add to the nutritional value of your salads.

Bonus Recipes

Recipe #10 Herbal Coconut Smoothie

This recipe is very soothing and relaxing. It's especially recommended as an afternoon or evening smoothie.

Serves 1-2
Ingredients:

- 1 teaspoon of Ashwagandha powder
- 1 cup of any herbal tea of your choice (for example mint, fennel, chamomile), cooled down
- 1 frozen banana, peeled
- 1 apple, peeled and diced
- 6 dates, pitted
- Half cup of blueberries
- Half teaspoon of lime juice

Instructions:

1. Place all the ingredients in a blender.
2. Process until smooth.
3. Serve and enjoy!

Connect with Karen

Connect with Karen

In Conclusion

Thank you for reading this recipe book to the end.

I hope that with so many vegan recipes you will feel inspired to take positive action on your vegan wellness journey.

The beauty of incorporating nutritious vegan foods into your daily diet is that you are making simple, yet sustainable changes that will work for your health and wellbeing, long-term.

If you enjoyed my book, it would be greatly appreciated if you left an honest review so that others can receive the same benefits you have. Your review can help other people take this important step to take care of their health and inspire them to start a new chapter in their lives.

I'd be thrilled to hear from you. I would love to know your favorite recipe(s).

➔ Questions about this book? Email me at: karenveganbooks@gmail.com

Thank You for your time,
Love & Light,
Until next time-
Karen Vegan Greenvang

Connect with Karen

Special Offer from Karen- VIP Reader Newsletter

Are you looking for more vegan health inspiration?

Join my free email newsletter today and start receiving my best vegan tips, recipes and resources:

Visit:

www.YourWellnessBooks.com/karen

to sign up now.

(As my VIP reader, you will be the first one to learn about my new books at super discounted prices + giveaways +discounts).

Join now, it's free:

www.YourWellnessBooks.com/karen

I am looking forward to connecting with you and sending you a surprise gift as soon as you sign up.

Connect with Karen

More Books Written by Karen Greenvang

Pegan Diet Cookbook

Alkaline Vegan Drinks

Vegan Baking

Spiralizer Cookbook

Vegan Protein Smoothies & Green Smoothies

And many more available at:

www.amazon.com/author/karengreenvang

Connect with Karen

Karen's email is:

karenveganbooks@gmail.com

Connect with Karen

www.ingramcontent.com/pod-product-compliance
Lightning Source LLC
Chambersburg PA
CBHW071748080526
44588CB00013B/2191